D1218897

BRITAIN IN PICTURES
THE BRITISH PEOPLE IN PICTURES

BRITISH CARTOONISTS
CARICATURISTS AND COMIC ARTISTS

GENERAL EDITOR

W. J. TURNER

*

The Editor is most grateful to all those who have
so kindly helped in the selection of illustrations,
especially to officials of the various public
Museums, Libraries and Galleries, and
to all others who have generously
allowed pictures and MSS.
to be reproduced

BRITISH
CARTOONISTS
CARICATURISTS AND COMIC ARTISTS

DAVID LOW

WITH
8 PLATES IN COLOUR
AND
29 ILLUSTRATIONS IN
BLACK & WHITE

WILLIAM COLLINS OF LONDON
MCMXXXXII

PRODUCED BY
ADPRINT LIMITED LONDON

*

PRINTED
IN GREAT BRITAIN BY
WILLIAM BROWN AND CO. LTD. LONDON

LIST OF ILLUSTRATIONS

PLATES IN COLOUR

THE ASSEMBLY ROOMS, BATH
Drawing by Thomas Rowlandson

'THE THREE JOVIAL HUNTSMEN'
Drawing by R. Caldecott
From Caldecott's *Collection of Pictures and Songs*

'THE SCAPEGOAT'
Cartoon by *Cynicus*
From *Cartoons Social and Political*, 1893

ALGERNON CHARLES SWINBURNE
Caricature by Carlo Pellegrini (*Ape*)
From *Vanity Fair*, 1874

JOHN HENRY NEWMAN
Caricature by Leslie Ward (*Spy*)
From *Vanity Fair*, 1877

'DANTE GABRIEL ROSSETTI, IN HIS BACK GARDEN'
Caricature by Sir Max Beerbohm
*The group includes Swinburne, Watts Dunton, Whistler,
William Morris and Mrs. William Morris, Hall Caine,
Dante Gabriel Rossetti and others*
From *The Poets' Corner*.   William Heinemann, 1904

'THE MAN WHO LIT HIS CIGAR BEFORE THE ROYAL TOAST'
Drawing by H. M. Bateman

'THE PAST MEETS THE PRESENT: JUBILEE DAY ON OLYMPUS'
Cartoon by David Low
*The gathering includes such well-known gods as Ramsay
MacDonald, Bernard Shaw, Wells, Maxton, Reith,
Beaverbrook, Lloyd George, Barrie, Churchill and C. B.
Cochran; also, some obscure—and perhaps legendary—
young men*

BLACK & WHITE ILLUSTRATIONS

Illustrations on pp. 17, 21, 23, 27, 28, 29, 34, 38, 39 reproduced
by courtesy of the Proprietors of *Punch*.

'ZIG-ZAG SIMIAN'
A Zoological caricature by J. A. Shepherd

IT is widely supposed that the English have a sense of humour but no sense of wit. There are, of course, some Englishmen under the impression that wit pointed against the things they disapprove or disdain is humour, and wit pointed against the things they approve or respect is offensive vulgarity. These strongly prefer what they think is humour, and deplore the other thing. There are others who hold that in all arts only performances possessing qualities of taste and refinement are worthy, and discourage the more robustious forms of wit found in the art of caricature as " un-English." During the last century the changes in the mood or temper of British wit and humour, which correspond to fluctuations in manners and modes, have for so long conformed to the standards of such tender souls that it might have seemed that these standards were eternal, and that England had always been more appreciative of the comic in its refined aspect as pleasantry rather than as mordancy with an edge. Hence, partly from a domestic misunderstanding among some of the English themselves, a curious misapprehension has arisen in the wider world about the people of a country which was once called the Home of Caricature and is historically the cradle of the cartoon as it is universally known to-day.

7

There is plenty of evidence of pictorial satire in England before William Hogarth, " Shakespeare of the etching needle," began painting and engraving his " modern moral subjects ", early in the eighteenth century. Engraved illustrations to pamphlets published in the time of Charles the First, for instance, displayed the spirit of caricature to such an extent that the unappreciative monarch was moved to anger against " these Madde Designes." The Civil War and its aftermath produced a harvest of political picture-satires, clumsy and crude. But before Hogarth there was no indigenous national caricature. It was an imported article and the local attempts were but stumbling imitations of the Italians and the Dutch. Hogarth, as much influenced as any of his contemporaries, was the first to infuse a characteristically English spirit into his practice of the art, and thus to found an English school distinct from the other schools on the Continent.

It is to the purpose here to comment only upon that part of Hogarth's work which is relevant to the development of the modern art of the cartoon. Of the rest let it suffice to say that he was a versatile painter who found himself at times unable to support his household. He was unwilling to become a mere manufacturer of portraits and conversation-pieces ; so he turned to a brave new idea. Both writers and painters in the historical style, he thought, had totally overlooked that intermediate species of subjects which may be placed between the sublime and the grotesque. Here was a field unexploited in any country or any age. He began painting and engraving what he called " modern moral subjects," and found at last a steady income in the sale of prints which he engraved from those that struck popular fancy.

" Thus did he shine," as Horace Walpole said, " in a field untrodden before. The curtain was drawn aside, and his genius stood displayed in its full lustre. From time to time he continued to give those works that should be immortal if the nature of his art will allow it."

The ideal of moral rectitude which inspired the caricaturists of the Middle Ages still hung about Hogarth when he founded the first indigenous school of English pictorial satire. So he became a heavyweight opponent of wickedness in general. " It was his business to arrest the thoughtless in their hasty steps to evil—to confirm the prudent in their steady march towards good," says a commentator. His was not the art of the rapier, but of the tank.

The two plates *Gin Street* and *Beer Street* are excellent examples of Hogarth's temper, the first indicting the curse of gin, the second applauding the blessing of beer ; the one heaped up with dreadful misery, the other with equally dreadful happiness. His most celebrated works are the successive sets of prints, *The Rake's Progress*, *The Harlot's Progress*, *Marriage à la Mode*, and others, each being a serial sermon, mostly of the hell-and-damnation variety. Virtue triumphs over Vice with sickening monotony, the Good Man always finishing up as Lord Mayor of London, the Bad Man always being publicly hanged at Tyburn.

THE ASSEMBLY ROOMS, BATH
Drawing by Thomas Rowlandson

'THE THREE JOVIAL HUNTSMEN'
Drawing by R. Caldecott
From Caldecott's *Collection of Pictures and Songs*

Alas ! times and tastes have changed, and we cannot swallow our morality so neat nowadays. Such violence to the emotions is apt to appear to us childish. But to judge the works of Hogarth by standards of subsequent development in the art of which he was a pioneer, is to look back at him through the wrong end of the telescope. Hogarth's pictures, in modern setting and printed in a modern periodical, would be called "cartoons," though certainly there is little in common with the conventions, either conceptual or technical, of to-day's cartooning in, say, *Suicide of the Countess, The Rake in the Madhouse, The Funeral.* "These prints are calculated to reform some reigning vices," announced the advertisement.

His first intention was to produce tableaux of life, pictures similar to representations on the stage. The probability that his public were unresponsive to demands upon the imagination and preferred to call a spade a bloody shovel accounts for the fact that there is about his compositions a theatrical rather than a dramatic effect, the details and accessories building up the point of an idea until it rants. A sophisticated modern cartoonist might justly criticise his way of littering his pictures with symbolism, and hold it to be overdoing the obvious to underline the same point several times over in the pictures hanging on the wall and the pattern on the carpet. The exaggeration in Hogarth's drawings is not always discriminating, of the kind which illuminates and explains. Often his humour was for the elementary souls who thought deformity amusing. Though he was capable of *The Cockpit* and *The Bench*, both plates displaying types which obviously ring true, he could also perpetrate the "comic" *Laughing Audience*, which to civilised people is not comic at all, but only ugly.

Such criticism may be made from 1942 without diminishing Hogarth's stature as one of the four Old Masters of caricature and cartooning—Brueghel, Hogarth, Gillray, Daumier. These four had the differences of their respective nationalities ; and each had, further, the marked individuality which distinguishes an original from all others of his kind. But Hogarth, the heavily realistic Englishman, like Brueghel, the droll slow Fleming, Gillray, the mocking ribald Scot, and Daumier, the emotional angry Frenchman, had breadth of vision and the intelligence to digest what he perceived and to make it his. His productivity, like that of the other three, was great, and he worked on the wide canvas with a zest and exuberance which may be discerned even to-day flowing as an undercurrent to the conscientious technique of his draughtsmanship.

Hogarth always insisted that he was no "caricaturer," but he understood the word not as we do to-day, but in the Italian sense then fashionable, as meaning a maker of trick likenesses. To him caricature was not an art of calculated and balanced exaggeration of individual characteristics, but an amusing aberration consisting of drawing the features of persons "with any sort of similitude in objects absolutely remote in their kind," an old boot, say, or a chair, a mountain, the sun or what-not. Hogarth was himself not particularly good at this pastime, though he made at least one " caricature " which was greatly admired, of a famous musician as a note of music. When he essayed the expression of character not by this inventive ingenuity but by the exaggeration of visible realities, his portraits of his great contemporaries were not far removed from normal accuracy. His portraits of *Simon, Lord Lovat* and *John Wilkes*, for instance, might hang in any historical gallery as faithful representations by an artist of unusual perception and freedom of execution, if, in the latter case, allowing himself a rather ill-expressed spite. Perhaps had Hogarth had an inkling of what we mean to-day by " cartooning " he would have insisted also that he was no " cartooner." Nevertheless it was the example of his work in the new field of his own development that most inspired the succeeding generation of engravers and subject-etchers. He was the grandfather of modern cartooning. Among his artistic progeny were Gillray and Rowlandson, its fathers.

Of these two the more significant figure is Gillray. Here at last is a worthy draughtsman to whom satire was a whole-time job and not a sideline. If Brueghel had raised caricatural draughtsmanship to the dignity of being a distinct art, and Hogarth had established a peculiarly English form of pictorial satire with moral purpose, Gillray took that art, form and purpose and fashioned them into something recognisably related to the modern cartoon. Hogarth's prints had been usually impersonal, and on those rare occasions when he touched upon politics the snobbish contempt for democracy which peeped through some of his drawings, and the Rule-Britannia-and-Damn-the-French air of others, indicated that he accepted the current conventions in political prejudice without much concern. Gillray, on the other hand, was a born politician, with a keen interest in the individuals who ' made the wheels go round.' His satirical turn was naturally more incisive and particular than that of Hogarth, because his aim was narrower and he occupied himself with more ephemeral aspects of his subjects. He specialised in personal portraiture and became an expert in the kind of draughtsmanship suited to the expression of his own sharp wit. Although his manner appears now old-fashioned, his approach to social and political satire is akin to that of the modern cartoonist. With Gillray we see developing the familiar technique of our own times—the selection of " characters " and their establishment as regular butts to be represented over and over again in different shapes and images of fantasy.

Gillray was no hireling, no servile champion of a faction. Even when under the influence of the spirit of war he grew the orthodox one-eyed passion against the foe, he remembered to remain the critic, not the servant, of authority. He was patriotic, but his was not the shallow patriotism which pretends that everything in the garden is lovely. On the contrary, many things seemed wrong to Gillray. The overstrained Royal prerogative, the political and legislative abuses, the disposition of Society to excessive gambling, sexual promiscuity and drunkenness, all provided him with material. The tolerance of the Government and the freedom of the Constitution gave him his opportunity.

GIN LANE
Moral engraving by William Hogarth, 1697-1764

He directed his wit with such daring independence that each of his caricatures took on an air of fresh surprise, not to say of astonishing impudence. He made many caricatures on the morals of the Royal court, on King George III himself, his meanness and his clumsy behaviour; on the Heir to the Throne, his expensive habits and his money troubles, his voluptuousness and his carryings-on with Mrs. Fitzherbert and other favourites. Perhaps the boldest pictorial parody ever published was his *Sin, Death and The Devil*, based upon Milton's immortal epic, in which the Queen appeared as the devil.

Within a short distance of the metropolitan palace of the King of England such satires were to be bought at the print-shop of Mistress Humphrey in Piccadilly for eighteen-pence apiece, while Gillray himself sat in his little room overhead etching fresh ones. Sometimes great commotion was caused outside, but usually the artist moved about without let or hindrance, and the shop windows were broken only once. The caricatures were regularly conveyed to Court, where their Majesties are reported to have expressed the opinion that those which opposed them were very poor and those which favoured them were very, very amusing.

Gillray, who favoured principles of freedom, at first approved of the French Revolution, but the execution of Louis and the works of the Terror were too much for him. The French threat of the invasion of England gave to his works, as to those of his contemporaries of that period, the special ill-will of a prejudice inspired by the common fear. A typical example is the rather bad cartoon which he drew showing Napoleon's head on a pike waved by a gloating John Bull, an indication of what would be the result of the threatened invasion. "We owe to Gillray's universal language of picture . . . much of that returning spirit of loyalty which ultimately preserved the country from invasion," wrote an historian. The battle of Waterloo was not won exclusively on the playing-fields of Eton.

As may be expected in the case of a figure who furnished the predominant subject-matter for satire for over a decade, Napoleon had a painful, if picturesque, time at Gillray's hands. When not a baby-eating cannibal, or a mongrel pup with tin-cans tied to his tail, he was a fox, a dragon, or supper for the devil. "Boney's" followers had their share of attention, notably Talleyrand, his Foreign Minister, who had a club-foot which made it easy for English caricaturists to confer immortality upon him as "Hopping Tally."

Napoleon's wife Josephine appears at first as a thin, ill-favoured creature, and later as a fat strumpet of the Drury Lane variety. One of the more ungallant caricatures of that ungentlemanly period was *Ci-Devant Occupation*, illustrating a rumour that Josephine and Madame Tallien had danced naked for the amusement of Barras, detailing in the caption below the unsavoury bargain that it was alleged had been struck between Napoleon and Barras regarding the former's "taking over" Josephine. In the caricature a bloated, leering Barras lolls back drunkenly while before him prance the nude ladies; Napoleon peers cautiously through the curtain at the scene. The whole composition is calculated to make the persons depicted see red.

Too much has been said and written about Gillray's indecencies. The most complete collection of his work is that which is considerately published in two large folios—one thick containing respectable prints, the other thin and comparatively unrespectable. It is natural that the crudeness of the popular taste of his day should be reflected in its due proportion. Gillray's treatment ranged from the heroic to the broadly comic, but his excesses at either extreme are excused to the discerning student because of the presence of that relevant satire which distinguishes caricature from crude foolishness. His caricature of Mr. Pitt as the bottomless Pitt, literally, excusing to the Commons a Fundamental Deficiency in the Treasury, a print of which hangs in the Mother of Parliaments, is a classic example of pertinent wit. When Gillray

'THE PLUMB-PUDDING IN DANGER: OR, STATE EPICURES TAKING *UN PETIT SOUPER*'
Caricature of Pitt and Napoleon carving up the globe
Engraving by James Gillray, 1805

illustrated his suspicion that Fox and others were inclining towards the advanced ideas of the French revolutionary sans-culottes, by drawing them always without any trousers, he produced " vulgarity " but not silliness. Fox was much incensed.

It is unfortunate that this ribaldry in a small number of Gillray's caricatures tends to frighten away the delicate-minded from the choicer examples of his skill in other moods. At his best he was a master of the peculiar technique of draughtsmanship necessary for caricature, in its full range from majestic allegory to topical skit. Nowadays of course many of his vaster plates—*The Apotheosis of Hooche*, for instance, teeming with grimacing figures and hideous cherubim, in the centre of which sits the hero playing a lute which is a guillotine—seem too crowded and suffocating ; and the device, often used, of conveying the full point of the idea in enormous legends covering half the picture, balloons full of writing coming from the mouths of the figures and zig-zagging down the margins, seems tiresome to the eye of 1942. But in general his compositions were well-judged and full of novelty, and his portraits remarkably illuminating and convincing. George III, Pitt, Canning, Burke, live in his caricatures much more vividly than in their conventional historical portraits, for he had the true caricaturist's instinct not only for expressing in exaggerated terms physical characteristics, but also for using the physical to express the spiritual.

Gillray developed intemperate habits and went off his head at a comparatively early age. His final appearance is full of a grotesque drama which itself suggests caricature. He unsuccessfully attempted suicide from the window of his room above Mistress Humphrey's print-shop in Piccadilly where his drawings were on sale, and then startled the customers by stalking into the shop naked. After that he died. A moody man, solitary even in company, was this acknowledged Prince of Caricaturists, who for twenty years had " partially guided, partially formed, and generally reflected the convictions of the many." His influence in the development of his singular art has been enduring and world-wide.

As a political caricaturist, William Rowlandson imitated the Gillray manner, method and boldness in attack, but in this métier he was far behind Gillray. Rowlandson was an inveterate gambler who was ruined and forced to work for a living, and he had not much interest in politics or public affairs. His tastes led him naturally to prefer the study of passing pleasures, sentiments and fashions. A tavern scene inspired him more than a political situation. Woman in all her conditions intrigued him more than Liberty. His caricatures gave women a rough classification : charming young girls, graceful and elegant : and fat old libidinous, blown-out, dropsical rouées. When he takes us under the shadows of Vauxhall among the tarts he is the most sprightly of the caricaturists of his time, but very low and very impudent. His crowds in Hyde Park, his Bath assemblies, are vivid contemporary records, rowdy but essentially true. His caricatures about food won immediate success in that England of which a centre of interest was then the stomach. These were, of course, the days of the three-bottle-men of the Regency. It was the custom for satirists to be ribald, and both Gillray and Rowlandson were but English in this respect. It is obviously easier to achieve mere grossness than discriminative exaggeration carefully balanced to illuminate an idea ; and Rowlandson was more pointlessly sensual than Gillray. But, at his best, in his own particular domain as a caricaturist of life and character, he was the better artist. In the more serious departments of drawing he was a splendidly sympathetic rich draughtsman. The romantic touch and the peculiarly native charm he captured in his broad renderings of English landscape made a permanent impression upon painters and draughtsmen and won him respect as a master.

Before Gillray's unhappy end in 1815 he occasionally started drawings which he was unable to finish. Often these had to be finished for him by others. Among these others were the youthful George Cruikshank and his brother Robert.

At first the brothers Cruikshank were closely associated and it is probable that many early drawings were the joint work of both ; but later they separated and came to the point of quarrelling with each other about their respective

'THE CRINOLINE RACE: OR, WHAT IT MUST COME TO AT LAST IF THE LADIES GO ON BLOWING
THEMSELVES OUT AS THEY DO'
Drawing by George Cruikshank

rights to sign with the plain surname " Cruikshank." Since, owing to this dispute, the brothers often would omit to sign their drawings at all, it is occasionally hard to identify the work of either except by a careful study of style and technique.

Difficulty in this respect is not lessened by the fact that George was an obliging fellow without any political conscience, ready not only to draw to order squibs against any policy, person or thing that could pay him his fee, but also to build up compositions of draughtsmanship from the " roughs " supplied by friends and clients, and to etch on the plates designs which were completely the work of other artists.

Robert was a fairly efficient caricaturist, more prolific in this line than George ; but no genius. George, it appears, started in to draw vigorous and occasionally indecent political and social caricatures in a manner which suggested strongly the influence of Gillray. He became " the clown in white gloves " working for the masses, specialising in brutal frankness. Even Gillray might have felt the Cruikshank *Life of Napoleon* went too far. George had a lively time in a riotous journal called *The Scourge*, which printed several caricatures which would be good for a term of imprisonment for criminal libel in our more tender days. He took the princesses' part against the Regent and gave it hot to Canning, Castlereagh, Bexley and Sidmouth. He had attracted considerable attention with a series of satires about the manners and customs of the Court when suddenly these ceased and the whole atmosphere of his work changed.

15

It was generally said—and not denied—that George's abandonment of the more downright kind of caricature was due to a tip he had received from Windsor Castle. True or not, a reaction had begun against " coarseness " and it is probable that George, always obliging, found it both more profitable—and congenial—to enter more genteel provinces of art. He became a book illustrator, at which his peculiar gifts of fancy caused him to be a great success; when he was not fighting his authors and quarrelling with his publishers— which happened constantly because of his theory that the illustrations should be drawn first at the unfettered discretion of the artist, the stories being written later to fit. From time to time the spirit of caricature gleamed, rather than shone, in his constant flow of quips about controversial topics ; but finally it gave place almost completely to that of innocent fun about such subjects as the weather, sport, the fashions, the danger of travelling in " these 'ere new-fangled railways," Christmas pudding, and the like. It is by this phase of his work that Cruikshank is best remembered : for the rounded humour of his genial outlook upon the little things of everyday life, and for the true Cockney flavour of his fancy. The panorama he left of the manners and modes of his times are part of the historical records of Britain.

Cruikshank (Robert had disappeared and George now enjoyed full title to the surname), who had lived a lusty youth, came in middle life to look upon his art as an instrument in the cause of uplift, with special reference to temperance. Unfortunately, as he waxed in his crusading fervour he waned as an artist. Years before, facile critics, admonishing him for a certain feebleness in conception, had urged him to think of Hogarth. Such a subject as the evils of Gin was, of course, eminently suitable to the art of Hogarth himself. Like a gloomy elephant having a bath, Hogarth would have lowered himself into it and wallowed.

But Cruikshank's line was too light, his imagination not robust enough for a second Hogarth. His monumental effort, *The Worship of Bacchus*, now reposing in the morgue for dead pictures under the National Gallery, is a mass composition of too many ideas closely drawn and so assembled as to be a weariness to the eye. His public yawned, and turned to other gods. Poor George ! After thirty years he attempted a come-back, but a new public had grown up which knew him not.

The growth of politeness in 1830 may be measured by the diminution of satire found in the political lithographs of *HB*, otherwise John Doyle. Doyle was a portrait painter who had an ability—not a facility—for drawing recognisable but rather dull likenesses of contemporary statesmen in postures and situations which were not too hard on their dignity. Of his subjects, which included Wellington, Peel, Melbourne, Derby and Russell, he was most successful with Brougham, who had a powerful face which almost drew itself. Restrained in temper and hesitant in line, *HB's* prints observed standards of decorum which are foreign to the tradition of caricature. After all, the business of a caricaturist is caricature. Doyle's publishers felt this and always called

'THIS IS THE BOY WHO CHALKED UP *NO POPERY*—AND THEN RAN AWAY!'
A cartoon by John Leech of Lord John Russell "asserting the Supremacy of the Crown"
at the time of the "Papal Aggression" disputes

them "Political Sketches." Perhaps *HB's* most valuable achievement was his son Richard, "Dicky" Doyle, who became a comic artist of much greater range.

Times and tastes were changing. In England caricature had had a very free time during the Napoleonic episode. But, apart from the evolution in manners, changes were taking place in the modes of producing and publishing caricatures which were to have far-reaching effects upon the whole future of graphic satire, its forms, conventions and temper. Wood-engraving began to supersede copper-plate etching. The copper-plate etchers had been usually the artists themselves, who, having drawn their pictures, carried them through the entire process of reproduction personally, often adding to and improving upon them as they went along. But in wood-engraving the personal touch became rarer and finally disappeared altogether. It was a quicker and cheaper process than etching. Accordingly floods of caricatures of indifferent quality, mostly anonymous, made their appearance. Caricatures dropped in price from a shilling to a penny. Greater simplicity and speed of reproduction foreshadowed a significant change. Caricature was to be taken under the wing of the press.

In 1841, the success of the French satirical weekly paper, *Charivari*, inspired in Britain the birth of *Punch*. The latter was announced as a comic paper "without grossness, partisanship, profanity, indelicacy, or malice." After the usual struggles it found its feet, and several promising caricaturists rose to the opportunity. The most notable was John Leech ; who, by the way, has the distinction, with Jerrold his editor, of being the first to apply the word " cartoon " to the graphic satires previously called caricatures.

In 1843 was held a great exhibition of rough designs, or " cartoons " (in the correct sense of the word), for the frescoes to be executed on the walls of the Houses of Parliament. It was an obvious opportunity. Leech caricatured these " cartoons " in a series of biting satires. The public remembered the word " cartoon " and has clung to it ever since.

Leech had a ready flow of ideas of his own. He had started drawing what *Punch* called " pencillings," which were not unduly cramped by the official abjuration of grossness, partisanship, profanity, etc. His earlier work was often sharply pointed. These were the stormy days of the " papal aggression " dispute, and Leech bitterly ridiculed the Pope and the Catholic Bishops. The Prime Minister, Lord Russell, had introduced his anti-Catholic Ecclesiastical Titles Bill, apologetically explaining that it was only a gesture. Leech drew his famous *No Popery* cartoon of Russell on Cardinal Wiseman's doorstep. It made a great stir and was said to have substantially aided Russell's fall shortly after. He disliked Jews, and at the time of the Jewish Disabilities Removal Bill he caricatured Baron de Rothschild trying to force his nose between the doors of the House of Commons, the title reading, *The Thin End of the Wedge*. His most aggressive satire was reserved, however, for foreigners, especially Frenchmen. Prince Louis Napoleon came in for spirited attacks, and Leech offended the susceptibilities of the whole French army with a celebrated caricature, *Cock-a-doodle-do*. On two occasions *Punch* was officially excluded from France—with Leech's help. The home statesmen were not exempt. Leech went for Brougham, Bright, Aberdeen, and especially Disraeli, firmly snubbing the ingratiatory advances of the latter, who appreciated his importance enough to court him personally, but without appreciable effect. Nor did the British lion himself enjoy a close season, but, during certain unhappy dealings with Greece, was presented as a sneaking, grovelling, delapidated quadruped, with *Punch* holding him by the ear and saying, " Why don't you hit someone your own size ? "

The famous Graham envelope was designed by Leech. Mr. Graham, the then Home Secretary, was alleged to have opened some private letters in the exercise of his official privilege. Leech drew a neat design of steaming kettles, Paul Prys, and snakes in the grass, which was printed on envelopes and had an immense sale for use through the post. Mr. Graham was effectively cured of his paternalism.

Punch prospered and gained circulation. He became *Mr. Punch*, with the added responsibilities and restraints that go with a widening circulation. His satire was scrutinised and the subjects of his cartoons debated by a vigilance committee of the staff, which included partisans of all current political faiths. When these subjects had been passed through the fire of controversy, singed of offence and passed as agreeable to everybody, they were, as might be expected, extremely fair-minded. Leech was more gentle in nature than Gillray, and his cartoons gradually lost the aggressive spirit which had filled his early pencillings. He was encouraged to avoid caricature. His serious compositions were hailed enthusiastically as his best. A heavily dramatic cartoon entitled *General Février Turns Traitor*, published at the time of the Crimean War, was said to be his high-watermark. The Emperor of Russia had been counting upon the icy blasts of the month of February to give him the advantage over his foes ; but he himself was struck down by illness during that month and died suddenly. This situation Leech illustrated by drawing the Czar lying dead upon his bier while a fearsome skeleton dressed in the uniform of a general rested an icy finger upon his heart. A heavily dramatic idea, adequately drawn, with plenty of snow and gloomy background. " Just think," said Leech's friends, forgetting much, " how savage Gillray or vulgar Rowlandson would have handled such a theme. They would have caricatured it."

Since Leech was the master hand, his imitators followed. " Serious " cartoons were more frequent, and cartoons in general became less infused with mockery. Satire was diffused into repartees and jokes, and Leech himself specialised in jokes about the hunting field and deer-stalking in the Highlands. His series of the adventures of *Mr. Briggs*, which, by the way, reveals that creation to be an ancestor of the modern comic strip, has a broad humour but appears innocent of any satirical motive, except perhaps to those persons who see in every perversion of the human shape a satirical comment upon the existence of the Race. After carrying on a decorous campaign against the wearing of bloomers by ladies, Leech devoted himself to the perfecting of a pretty girl's head—the " Leech girl "—for which he won great popularity. The political powers, no doubt grateful for his mildness, comforted his declining years with a pension.

Leech's contemporaries included a young man, John Tenniel, destined to become a landmark in British cartooning. He confirmed Leech's latter-day code of good behaviour for cartoonists. Indeed he may be said to have created upon it, to rival the original Gillray tradition, a new Tenniel tradition, together with almost an " official " style for its expression.

He took Gillray's ribald *John Bull* and smoothed him down into a heavily dignified figure which evoked a comfortable feeling of satisfaction in the breasts of the great middle classes of 1860, who recognised their likeness immediately.

The idea of representing the national ego as a goddess was not, of course, Tenniel's, but it was he who took not only *Britannia* but the whole *Britannia* family on the permanent staff, so to speak, of Cartooning. The goddesses *Germania, Columbia, La Belle France, Russia, Erin* and the rest appeared engaged in lofty commerce one with another so frequently that they gradually created a world of their own. One lost sight of their symbolic mission and grew interested in them for their own sakes—in the sympathetic hand-clasps they would give one another in times of disaster ; the frigid glances when relations were strained ; the laurel wreaths they would place upon the tombs of one another's latest dead statesmen.

Tenniel, like other cartoonists of his day, worked straight on the surface of the wood-block later to be cut by the engraver. On this severely restricted space he drew his cartoons in reverse with a finely pointed hard lead pencil, making no direct use of models. The conditions were not conducive to enterprise in technical experiment, since so much had to be left to the engraver, who very often had his own ideas about how to interpret a shadow or a softness. But Tenniel himself was a sober draughtsman who made little attempt to render in line the different textures of materials. This gave his work a peculiar woodenness of technique which imparted an air of stiff dignity to whomever and whatever he drew. He gave the statesmen, whatever their politics, a stern unbending appearance which was no doubt gratifying to them, if tiresome to their critics. His portraits were, for the most part, unillumined, and not always up-to-date with the ageing appearance of their mortal originals. But such details need not obscure the fact that he had in his compositions largeness of conception and dramatic power which made his art peculiarly suited to the illustration of allegory.

The subject matter, points and parallels used by Tenniel were almost invariably selected for him by others. He took only a mild interest in what lay behind his drawings. We are told that during the discussions he made few remarks, but sat thinking not of the political or social but of the artistic possibilities of the subjects. The temptation to choose a novel idea good to draw, in preference to one sound in point but poor in pictorial promise, is always present to a cartoonist ; and the attraction of analogies suited to the Tenniel style but insufficiently apt to the circumstances of the occasion sometimes led to a confusion of meaning.

Strangely enough his most famous cartoon is an example of this. *Dropping the Pilot* shows the German Chancellor, Prince Bismarck, dressed as a pilot leaving the ship, the German Empire, while the Emperor leans over the bulwark regarding him. The point of the situation which evoked this cartoon was that Bismarck's dismissal was an astonishing and unexpected event, but the leaving of a ship by the pilot is a perfectly normal and expected event—in no way a real parallel. The cartoon, though, was successful. Both Bismarck and the Emperor were very pleased.

Tenniel is remembered almost exclusively for the cartoons of his later years, which were eminently well-bred. But his hard pencil was sharper-pointed and less well-behaved in his youth. His cartoons during the American Civil War were sharp enough to make the sympathisers of Abe Lincoln wince. His art, mellowing early, achieved and maintained a high standard of gentlemanly decorum. He was discretion itself in producing powerful cartoons that offended

'GOD SAVE THE QUEEN!'
Cartoon by John Tenniel celebrating the Jubilee of Queen Victoria, 1887

nobody. Upon a tight place arising in foreign diplomacy, for instance, he would draw the British Lion gazing nobly at the horizon with his front paw resting on a document, a gun or a rock, as the occasion suggested. He would skate around the point of a sore political controversy with sufficient tact and ambiguity to avoid embarrassment, finding a playful parallel to the situation in *Alice in Wonderland* or *Pickwick Papers* ; or depicting both sides posing nobly in armour with a wealth of historical appearance in a cartoon accompanied by a column of poetry.

Tenniel's was a great personal triumph. His work stretching over nearly half a century constitutes a history in pictures—a history of Victorian affairs from a typical Victorian viewpoint. It was generally felt by his admirers that his cartoons bore some relationship to, but were an improvement on, caricatures —something more refined. But speaking generally, the spirit pervading Tenniel's work was the opposite of the Gillray spirit of caricature. Tenniel was Dignity, not Impudence. If his work sometimes had the defect of its great qualities—a failing in crude force when crude force was required—he neverthe- less brought to the whole art of cartooning a respectability which must have astonished the shades of Gillray and Rowlandson. He became an institution and his talents were recognised with a knighthood before he died, honoured at home and abroad.

On Tenniel's death, his mantle gracefully descended upon the shoulders of Linley Sambourne, who, in actual fact, had been wearing already a capacious robe of his own for some years previously. It is said that Sambourne was

21

'MR. PUNCH'S NOTES—IN CORRECT TIME
Drawing by Linley Sambourne

rather proud of being able to draw a perfect circle freehand. One cannot expect a graphic artist, engrossed in the properties of the objects he is representing, to be as unconscious of his own manipulation as a healthy man is unconscious of his body ; but Sambourne was perhaps too preoccupied with the technical business of making lines. He took great care to make his outlines all of the same thickness, to follow rounded surfaces with rounded lines, flat surfaces with flat lines, and so on. As a result his cartoons, impeccably drawn, often had a mechanical air suggestive of the engineering draughtsman's office at which Sambourne when young had served an apprenticeship.

'PULLED UP AT LAST'
P.C. Dizzy: "*It's no use, Sir. I've strict orders from the country not to let anything of the sort pass.*"
Caricature of Disraeli by W. Bowcher

Even so, he evolved a style which for sheer purity of line and solid correctness of draughtsmanship has not been excelled among British artists; a line which thereafter greatly affected the technique not only of British cartoonists but of black-and-white artists generally everywhere; and a meticulous accuracy which is a standing rebuke to that carelessness which is popularly supposed to belong to the artistic temperament.

In producing a continuous stream of drawings of assorted subjects— yesterday a locomotive, to-day a Chinese pagoda, to-morrow the inside of a piano—it is human for cartoonists to err occasionally. Tenniel did, Leech did, Gillray did, Hogarth did. But not Sambourne. Sambourne had a passion for accuracy which he allied to an enthusiasm for the (then) new hobby of photography. It is written that he prowled with his camera habitually. At his death he had 100,000 photographs of backgrounds, figures and details useful in drawing cartoons. The vicissitudes of *John Bull*, *Britannia* and the other cartoon myths were acted out on his back lawn and carefully photographed, later to be translated into the dignified symphonies in line signed " *Sambourne inv. et fec.*"

It should not be imagined, however, that Sambourne was a limited inventor, as this might suggest. On the contrary. He possessed a considerable talent for grotesque and caricature. In ornamental borders and initial letters—conventions of humorous art in his day—he poured forth from a crowded imagination intricate compositions full of detail carefully distorted

23

and harmoniously exaggerated. Though time has obscured their allusive wit and symbolic meaning, they remain models of excellent drawing ; but they pay the penalty of being too plentiful, too crowded together to be properly appreciated by casual observers. Even the best of cooks should not serve their tasty dishes in portions of a hundredweight.

The effect of his political cartoons was greatly strengthened by his talent for reliable portraiture. While he was not a great analyst of character—the long series of Fancy Portraits which he contributed to *Punch* have a static conventional quality suggesting a tiresome dependence upon his beloved photographs—his ringletted Disraelis, his Gladstones, Chamberlains and Harcourts, when they were once "run in," became lively caricatures, supple and workable in any expression from any angle. In his cartoons on foreign affairs may be traced the rise of aggressive Prussianism in Germany, and the decay of the Czardom in Russia. *The Release*, which depicts Liberty emerging from a Russian prison after the "constitutional changes" of 1905 ; and *The Eleventh Hour*, the shade of Louis XVI saying to the Czar, "Side with your people, sire, while there is yet time—I was too late," are but two examples of hundreds of simple, even obvious ideas given distinction by dramatic composition and masterly drawing. Sambourne made no one cartoon by which he is always remembered, as did Tenniel with his *Dropping the Pilot* ; but *The Tug of Peace*—heavily armed Germany, France, Russia and Britain inviting one another to enter the Temple of Disarmament first : "After you, sir "—is a famous work of his, the moral of which is still fresh. He was perhaps at his best in Tragedy. *Requiescat*, a heavily mournful cartoon drawn on the death of Queen Victoria, is unequalled in this vein.

During the reign of Leech, Tenniel and, latterly, Sambourne, their bright and continuous shine somewhat obscured the lesser lights of their rivals and imitators. Not to be ignored, however, is Matt Morgan, an artist of somewhat ponderous moralities on social injustice, more or less at home in the Hogarthian treatment of beautifully rounded but unhappy females, victims of the Wicked City, being fished out of the river ; and rather laboured political cartoons showing more of the same females labelled *Ireland* being betrayed by grim unshaven villains labelled *Fenian*, and extremely sturdy *John Bulls* being restrained by scoundrel politicians from giving treacherous *Uncle Sams* the father of an allegedly well-deserved hiding.

The nearest rivals to Tenniel were W. Bowcher and Gordon Thomson, cartoonists of *Judy* and *Fun* respectively. Both were competent draughtsmen, with sound pictorial sense and good at portraits. Cartooning in the 1870's was mainly devoted to the long political duel between Gladstone and Disraeli ; and Bowcher and Thomson harped on these two rich personalities. It is unfortunate for both artists, however, that they took usually too narrow an angle of vision for their works to endure. Bowcher's cartoons showing Mr. G. gazing Narcissus-like at his own reflection in a stream ; travelling in a broken-down cab pulled by a disreputable nag ; as the Grand Old Tinker mending

'THE SCAPEGOAT'
Cartoon by *Cynicus*

ALGERNON CHARLES SWINBURNE
Caricature by Carlo Pellegrini (*Ape*)

a battered pot—splendid drawings that they are—might be splendid cartoons, too, were they about great issues instead of ephemeral party squabblings. Occasionally, moved by burning issues now long dead, Bowcher launched thunderbolts of more verve and significance. His Mr. G. burning Protestant archbishops at the Stake; and burying Honour, Conscience and Reputation at dead of night (both inspired by Irish Church Disestablishment) have a lively mordancy. Bowcher gave Mr. G. a bad time. But there was always Gordon Thomson on the opposition periodical across the way to reply for the defence with a cartoon of Mr. G. as, say, William the Conqueror with his foot on Disraeli's chest.

A cut below Bowcher and Thomson were their respective successors, John Proctor and William Parkinson. Proctor was an imitator of Tenniel's manner, a more animated and varied draughtsman but far less of a cartoonist. His qualities are seen to better advantage in his illustrations to " Tim Pippen" and other children's books than in his rather pedestrian satires. Over-enthusiastic admiration of both Tenniel and Sambourne was the undoing of William Parkinson, who evolved a style reminiscent at odd times of both, in which he rendered correct but undistinguished cartoons at the expense of the inevitable Mr. G.

This account of the progress of British cartooning up to the time of its arrival in the daily newspapers might fittingly end with, as postscript, *Cynicus*. During the early '90's *Cynicus*, a Scot, himself published from his studio, cards and books of cartoons, social and political. They were coloured by hand and their broad simplicity of treatment had an attraction of its own despite defective draughtsmanship. Dealing in generalisations and never personal, *Cynicus* was a comprehensive and downright critic. No mealy-mouth he. Among his dislikes were Parliament, Democracy, Monarchy, Labour (The Brutish Working-Man), Capital, The Law, History, the Church, Speculators, Landlords, the Peerage, Vice, Politicians, and Journalism. Each subject was accompanied usually by a rhymed couplet in appropriately biting terms (*e.g.,* Journalism : " Gloating in gore and gruesome gabble, A paltry pimp who panders to the rabble.") The authentic latter-eighteenth-century spirit. A reminder that satire is not mere pleasantry.

THE COMIC ARTISTS

IN the revulsion of feeling from "coarseness" which came early in the nineteenth century, caricaturists metaphorically donned white kid gloves and tried to forget their ribald past. Artists became less interested in ideas, and more in excellence of draughtsmanship. Presently there appeared a succession of comic artists of high ability, masters of draughtsmanship who raised humorous drawing to a much higher level of artistry than formerly.

It is supposed by the ignorant that satire, wit and humour are interchangeable terms meaning the same thing. But obviously satire, though essentially witty, is not infrequently serious in intent and solemn in treatment, without a gleam of humour ; and, conversely, humour requires no wit nor satire to be first-rate as humour. The dividing line between the satirical and the humorous, however, especially when the form of expression is caricatural draughtsmanship—between, that is, the art which " overloads " with a critical purpose and that which " overloads " for mere amusement—is easily stepped over ; and many of the distinguished cartoonists have been also distinguished comic artists. The work of Cruikshank and Leech in this field have been mentioned already. The greatest of the British comic artists, Charles Keene, was, however, hardly a cartoonist or a caricaturist in the true sense at all.

Charles Keene, a reserved, modest, frugal man, son of a solicitor, was partial to old music (especially on the bag-pipes), old songs, old prints, old books, old flints, old clothes and very old clay pipes. He was an artist's artist, appreciated by his fellow draughtsmen and the knowing few, not specially distinguished by the wide public who incline to estimate the merits of an artist in the line of humour by the joke printed below the drawing. Keene was not, in fact, a humorist in the literary sense. Most of his jokes were supplied to him by friends. Neither was he the comic draughtsman of exaggeration. His was not the humour of invention, but of observation. He was supreme in " catching Nature in her humorous moments."

Working upon a foundation of scrupulously correct draughtsmanship from the life, Keene's genius as a comic artist lay in the warm geniality which he worked into the very lines of the finished drawing. He was influenced by the woodcuts of Menzel, his drawings were distinguished by broad and rich effects of light and shade, and had the restfulness which comes from complete unity. His chiaroscuro (that overworked term) was grand. Without straining truth, he produced a convincing panorama of the world as seen through the eyes of one who approved middle-class ideals, revered established institutions and resented change (especially among the " lower orders "), cordially disliked Irishmen and Americans. But though a man of strong, even childish, prejudices privately, these did not unnecessarily crop up in his drawings, for he avoided direct comment on his material. He occasionally put his cronies into his drawings but his talent in getting likenesses was negligible. His most important

'POLITESSE OBLIGE'

HANSOM CABBY (*suppressing a volley of imprecations at the tip of his tongue—the four-wheeler had narrowly grazed his horse's nose—as he'd a Lady inside*): " Pray, 'ow d'yer like London, Sir ? "

Drawing by Charles Keene

work was the illustrating of somewhat long-winded jokes, displaying delight-fully drawn flunkies, middle-class " old gents," parvenu rich, working-men M.P.'s, Church of England clergymen, snobs, waiters (his *Robert* was a creation) Highland gillies, and Irish peasants. The types he drew were not beautiful, elegant, nor well-groomed, like those of his contemporary Du Maurier ; and he could not draw pretty girls as could Leech. In fact, the inevitable fastidious boneheads, blind to his consummate artistry, complained sometimes that his works were " degraded," " obscene," and " odious."

Keene's drawings suffered more than most in process of reproduction because of his peculiar methods of work. He *would* draw, for instance, with bits of pointed wood and home-made inks of various shade and colours, producing soft touches and delicate subtleties which excite joy in admirers of his originals to-day, but which drove the patient wood-cut engravers of his time to deep profanity. He took dislikes to drawing papers and liked to use odd scraps with a nice grain, say, on the insides of old envelopes which he treasured for the purpose. A character, this lanky Carlo Keene, on the street corner making notes in a sketchbook with an ink-bottle tied to his waistcoat button.

Since the English are suspicious of originals and must have it always that so-and-so is " a second such-and-such," Keene began as the " successor of Leech " ; but he soon demonstrated that he was himself, and no successor to

'FELINE AMENITIES'

" Look, Dear ! There's your husband going in to supper with Mrs. Scudamore—a dangerously attractive woman.
Let me warn you ! "
" How good of you ! How I wish he was going in to supper with you, dear, instead ! "

Drawing by George du Maurier

anybody. It was in reality Du Maurier, a polished and graceful illustrator, who stepped into the shoes of Leech as the social satirist of *Punch*. Du Maurier was a transplanted Parisian who lost his Gallic lightness, yet his work remained more sentimental than satirical. He used the same very mannered inspiration and technical style for illustrating both serious novels and the social satires ; and the satire of the latter was generally contained only in the text beneath—which is, as they say, " something else again." A specialist in the polite touch, when he essayed comicality in line the results were uncomfortable. " Don't be funny," he was told, " do the refined side of life." Yet, despite the refinement, he often succeeded in conveying biting irony, mostly by the ancient device of creating " characters " and using them as butts. His *Sir Georgius Midas*, the parvenu, and *Mrs. Ponsonby Tompkins*, the social climber, did good service when the artist felt like using a more aggressive weapon than a feather. His *Cimabue Browns* came in very handy as the vehicle for a dirty right to the brisket of the " greenery-yallery " æsthete movement, which he cordially disliked. But Du Maurier's chief success lay in his pictures of handsome broad-shouldered men and elegant ladies of classic beauty, that so mightily pleased the middle classes who loved to think English Society was like that. This persistent representation of the contemporary

28

'WATER-WORKS'
Drawing by Phil May from *Guttersnipes*, 1896

female as a statuesque goddess was perhaps Du Maurier's most significant gift to his time ; for the effect of the subtle flattery stimulated Nature to imitate Art and it is alleged that in striving to live up to the ideal the average stature of the English girl increased by four inches.

The reputation of Randolph Caldecott rests mainly on his picture books for children, which he illustrated with such simple charm that they are remembered with affection as well as admiration by the children now grown to great-grandparents. He made also social pictures for the *Graphic*, convincing in character. In this work he was the pictorial equivalent of an exceptionally gifted descriptive-writer with an amiable humour. His work offers no criticism, makes no comment beyond something approximating to " You've got a nice day for it." He loved England, the out-of-doors and horses. He became a kind of national official portrayer of Christmas. In general his art displayed the good heart and kindly nature of the artist.

Caldecott was an original, independent, refusing steady work, irked by other people's suggestions. There have been many sounder draughtsmen, even in his own time, but none who could put on paper with such engaging simplicity the fresh sweetness of English fields and the clean air of English country. Perhaps only foreigners with an unaccustomed eye can properly appreciate

ALLY . . . .

this authentic local quality, flowing as naturally as with Moreland and Rowlandson if along different channels. Caldecott died at 40—the right age for a genius who would not outstay his welcome. His influence was not lost on succeeding generations.

In 1872 began a second revolutionary development in the mode of reproducing black-and-white drawings. Though many artists had achieved individuality of style during the days of wood-engraving, generally speaking all had had to work " with the wood " and their drawings could not escape a certain family resemblance imposed by the technique of the graver's tools. The perfecting of photo-process engraving, however, promised facsimile reproduction of their own actual lines to the smallest detail. Artists began to break away from wood-cut styles, to loosen up and to draw with more stylish originality. The new process had existed for some years when its most notable consequence occurred in Phil May.

Founding himself upon Linley Sambourne, whose work his early efforts closely resembled, May evolved a style of drawing which, by contrast with the laborious and closely-worked cross-hatched technique of the wood-cut school, charmed by its simplicity and apparent spontaneity. It has often been said that this evolution of style was necessitated by the poor quality of paper and printing of the Sydney *Bulletin* in Australia, where May worked for a few years in his youth. This is, however, untrue. May's Australian work, expertly engraved and well reproduced, appears comparatively tight and careful and the files show that he evolved his linear simplicity and nonchalance at a later date no doubt from purely artistic motives.

The influence of Phil May on English comic art is comparable to that of Caran D'Ache on the French—which is to say that " his inimitable pencil " (to use an expression dear to inexpert writers on this popular art in which barefaced imitation is so common) had more imitators than any of his contemporaries. But economy of means and smooth flow of line are not virtues by themselves. That May's dashed-off effects were carefully contrived is evident from a look at his painstaking preliminary studies of figure and composition. The essential quality of the May execution was its nerve. No one but a fellow artist who has actually tried it can tell of the peculiar bravery required to sacrifice all the careful detailed preliminaries and to slap in the bold lines. Phil May was not a good cartoonist, for he had no political sense and his drawings hardly ever had an objective moral. Neither was he a first-rate caricaturist of persons, though deft at catching a superficial resemblance. He never approached *Ape*, for instance, in the analysis, selection and emphasis of individual character. May's most famous portrait, that of Gladstone sitting on the Front Bench, masterpiece of expression that it is, full of life and repressed energy, discovers, one feels, qualities in the artist rather than in his subject.

Phil May's best known line was illustrated jokes. The convention made it necessary for his drawings to be accompanied by witticisms in text. With some artists these literary efforts were usually the essential kernel of the humour, but they mattered little to Phil May, being often just pegs on which to hang his drawings of types. For Phil May was mainly interested in types ; not so much particular individuals as kinds of people—the kinds of people one saw in the streets. He was lively, suggestive, and amusing, an excellent observer of generalised character, more observant of human variety than Keene, though much less of an artist in the broader sense, without ability to create a harmonious setting. Composition did not worry Phil May, for he did not worry it. Indeed his drawings often had no composition at all, being just two figures without background suspended in space—ill-assorted figures, too, sometimes drawn in different styles and different lights. Perhaps the artist was too easily seduced by the parts he found good to draw to put in the hard labour of unifying the whole. More likely, having magnified the elimination of the unnecessary to a supreme principle, he judged backgrounds to be superfluous.

Unlike most comedians of the pen, usually sedate and respectable citizens in private life, Phil May was a careless happy-go-lucky who wore check suits, picturesque fringe, smoked cigars, and enjoyed riotous company. Lived, in fact, as comic artists are supposed to live, but so rarely do. " Draw firm and be jolly," he said. Looking at his work in accumulation it is probable that social investigators of the future will account his period as one unusually rich with picturesque characters ; not realising that disposition of this artist to be attracted by the bits good to draw and to impart to them his own mood. Carping critical ghouls of the future may say that Phil May's drawings were shallow in that he made no psychological comment on his epoch. Those who must attach a profound psychological significance to the simplest act may have it that he had a sympathy with street urchins, on the strength of his having drawn them so often. Much more likely, he just found them jolly to draw. He was too interested in the varied

. . . . SLOPER
Drawings by W. G. Baxter

appearance of the animal, Man, to concern himself with its significance. That was not his job. At his job he was magnificent.

A simplicity like that of May, but quite different in quality, revealed itself in the drawings of J. A. Shepherd, a remarkably original caricaturist of animals. Not, mark you, a mere drawer of *funny* animals, but a true observer of their characteristics, with whom the prehistoric artist who drew the mammoth in the cave of Altamira might have shaken hands as a worthy descendant. He put his zoo on paper with a sweet line, delightful simplicity, understanding and dash. He, too, has had his imitators, but remains unique.

Leech, Du Maurier, Caldecott, May—these were comic artists of the three-penny and sixpenny " class " periodicals. But there were now, thanks to cheaper reproduction, many comic papers of lesser price and refinement. *Ally Sloper's Half-holiday* gave W. G. Baxter the opportunity to develop a character which became a national institution. *Ally*, whose paper ran on " family " lines with recurring gags and familiar characters week by week, appeared himself regularly on the front page in a kind of topical half-joke-half-cartoon, drawn with skill and a nice judgment of requirements by Baxter, and later by his successor, W. F. Thomas. The *Half-holiday* became the poor man's *Punch*. The masses, who never quite believed in *Britannia* or *John Bull*, understood perfectly *Ally Sloper*, that absurd figure with bulbous red nose, Micawber hat, baggy gamp, facetiousness and ribald slap-stick, and took him to their hearts.

Since the arts of cartoon, caricature and comic art are essentially of the people, it is fitting also that the merits be recognised here of such popular artists in picture-story as Oliver Veal, the father of the Ha'penny Comic strip, a genius whose eccentric creations had mouths that used to slip round to the backs of their necks when they got excited ; and the unknown inventors of Airy Alf and Bouncing Billy, and Weary Willie and Tired Tim, who were too modest to sign their mirthful works which so engaged the affections of youth in the early days of the present century.

JOHN HENRY NEWMAN
Caricature by Leslie Ward (*Spy*)

'DANTE GABRIEL ROSSETTI, IN HIS BACK GARDEN
Caricature by Sir Max Beerbohm

The group includes Swinburne, Watts Dunton, Whistler, William Morris and Mrs. William
Morris, Hall Caine, Dante Gabriel Rossetti and others.

THE PORTRAIT CARICATURISTS

SEVERAL times in the preceding pages I have distinguished between the ability to express ideas and the ability to draw caricatural likenesses of persons. In other words, between a cartoonist of situation and a caricaturist of personality. The two are by no means the same. Indeed, their arts can become quite different. It is sufficient usually for cartoonists to deal in generalised " likenesses " founded upon current already-created versions of what persons are like—whether these are resemblances in actuality or not ; but the study of individual particularity, involving the mental as well as the ocular vision, is the sine qua non of personal caricature.

It is not surprising, then, that caricaturists of personality are seldom cartoonists of situation, and vice versa. We have seen that Gillray was a brilliant exception to this generalisation in being excellent in both ; Rowlandson, an indifferent portraitist himself, borrowed Gillray's likenesses shamelessly ; Cruikshank's were mostly just comic portraits, possessing no true insight into character.

There is in existence at least one large canvas to show that Tom Patch, a cartoonist of minor merit in 1760–1770, had the proper idea, even though his attempts do not quite come off. Of more consequence was Robert Dighton, a portrait painter who early in the last century produced a gallery of etched caricatures in colour of Oxford celebrities. The Dighton manner was developed in 1862, when there began to appear in the weekly journal *Vanity Fair* a series of single figure caricatures of celebrities excellently printed in colour and with the authentic touch, a series which began what became later a national institution—the " *Vanity Fair* Cartoons." These were the work of a genius in his speciality, *Ape*—the pen-name of an Italian, Carlo Pellegrini. *Ape's* caricatures were maximum likenesses, that is to say they represented not only what he saw but also what he knew. Most of them to-day look as though they were probably more like the persons they depict than were those persons themselves.

Ape found some people harder to get than others, and he did not particularly like tracking down the difficult ones. So a new young artist, Leslie Ward, signing himself *Spy*, was set to crack *Ape's* hard nuts. A stern apprenticeship. When finally *Ape* had a disagreement with the proprietor of the journal in 1873, *Spy* slipped into his place.

Spy, who came of a family of artists, had had an orthodox art training which left him with a somewhat harder and less elastic equipment than his master. But, following the *Ape* style, he was a careful and conscientious worker who went to great trouble to gather his materials. " Distance frequently lends fictitious appearance to a face," he said, peering close under the whiskers of next week's subject. He followed his subject about many times to observe his manner of walking, noting closely his odd-shaped skull, his turn of wrist, the peculiar curl of his nostril, the unique droop of his eyelid, and so on. He would sit for hours in court memorising the features of a lawyer, or in church hunting a bishop in his pulpit. *Spy* frequently had sittings from willing subjects, but he learned to use his memory extensively in circumstances where subjects were unwilling and sketch-books were inconvenient. He held that personal idiosyncracies could only be discerned at first hand. As a result, his gallery is not a monotonous repetition of types, reeking of similarity, but a differentiation of individuals.

The popularity of the *Vanity Fair* type of caricature died, unfortunately, with the coming of the snapshot camera to surfeit the public with intimate views of celebrities. *Spy* tailed off latterly from true caricature into mere characteristic portraiture calculated to please the subjects, by hiding rather than by interpreting their irregularities.

The region of politics has always attracted caricaturists because the celebrities there are ready-made, offering themselves on a plate, so to speak.

'GETTING GLADSTONE'S COLLAR UP'
The first appearance of a famous piece of caricature by Harry Furniss

In 1880 arrived Harry Furniss, a versatile black-and-white artist who specialised in caricature portraits of politicians on their own stamping ground, as they lived and had their being. Harry Furniss was a facile—perhaps too facile—worker. Indeed, at his zenith he was almost a factory. Besides his three or four weekly portraits he produced frequent political cartoons, created a dainty " Furniss Girl," illustrated many books, a good number of which he wrote himself, went out on long lantern-lecture tours, started a couple of weekly papers, and in addition found time to be a busy man-about-town. He had vehement political views of his own, too, that sometimes obtruded themselves into his work. Had Furniss produced less he would have been accounted a better artist. But this pertinacious performer galloped too fast for his horse. He had too much energy, and he imparted it to his material. His figures had little repose. His style of execution, seen so often, became monotonous, even when applied to the caricature of other styles—a favourite trick of his—and his quick cleverness did not last. Nevertheless in perspective it is obvious that he was an unusually accomplished caricaturist able to represent—and misrepresent—individuals as he saw them, with a fancy pleasing and humorous if superficial. Harcourt's chins and Gladstone's collars are good examples of his invention, the latter a piece of caricature which became so celebrated that it passed into history with the statesman.

The successor to Harry Furniss as *Punch* Parliamentary caricaturist was E. T. Reed, who, on the other hand, had too much repose. Reed was primarily a comic artist, best remembered for his *Prehistoric Peeps* and humours of the law-courts. Purely as a portrait-caricaturist, his work wore the old-school-tie and was perhaps too careful of the dignity of the personages who were its raw material ; though when he had adjusted his style to the (then conventional) form of portrait-crammed cartoon, he was lively enough. His caricatures never aspired to

DAN LENO
Caricature by Ş. H. Sime

be other than amiable and amusing. Within their limitations—rather severe limitations upon the true art of caricature—he was usually competent and sometimes excellent.

All the caricaturists mentioned, some more than others, aspired to formal artistic qualities in their works. They conceived of " good drawing " as polished classical draughtsmanship, properly shaded, faultless in proportion and perspective. In the '90's, a decade fertile in adventurous talents impatient of tradition, there began to appear occasional caricatures by Max Beerbohm, *Max*. It was obvious that in the accepted sense *Max* could not draw at all.

35

MARIE LLOYD
Caricature by Henry Ospovat

His technique was naïve and almost childish. He appeared ignorant of the traditional clichés and formulæ. He side-stepped rather than overcame the problems of linear representation. But it was just as obvious that he had a lively wit. His free pencil, guided by his wit, proved, in fact, admirably suitable for the rendering of personal character, for it permitted to an unlimited extent the artistic sleight-of-hand involved in complete representation. There are certain guiding principles for expressing what can be seen, but there are none for expressing in graphic terms what can *not* be seen. In *Max's* best caricatures may be discerned an instinct discovering " the emotional elements of human form," and an artless ingenuity in adapting a propriety of thoughts and lines to the subject.

36

GEORGE MOORE
Wax model by Edmund Dulac

Max was (for though he still lives, his caricatures have ceased) a master of
the caricature situation and the caricature caption. It was in the combination
of his artistic and his literary wit that he reached his highest form as an
interpreter of character. His *Tout Seul se Rétablir*, for example, showing a
worried group including Hyndeman, Wells, Galsworthy, Sydney Webb,
Cunninghame Grahame and others, with the sub-caption, "Urgent conclave of
Doctrinaire Socialists to decide on some means of inducing the Lower Orders to
regard them once more as Visionaries only," contains all the elements of
good caricature.

But *Max* did not have the caricature of the '90's to himself. The theatre
usually has afforded a parade of personality, and during these years there grew

up a spate of theatrical caricaturists. The most notable was S. H. Sime, a beautifully imaginative artist, with a mordant fancy which sometimes overlaid his observation of character, but whose studies of people nevertheless are full of true and well-balanced caricature. No mere vulgar sprawling irresponsibility about him, but a patient individual appraisement in his own terms. A decade later was the droll Henry Ospovat, pre-occupied with the physical, which is in his case enough ; and, yet another decade, H. M. Bateman, whose romping caricatures of actors and his fellow artists show him to have a judgment of essentials.

Still living but, alas ! no longer caricaturing is Edmund Dulac, a careful exponent with a nice capacity for wedding style to subject. His Bernard Shaw in wood-cut is a finely executed reflection and his George Moore modelled in wax is the spirit (and, one is almost persuaded the body) of the man himself. In Dulac's work was a touch of *Max* plus a tender and orientally scrupulous artistry.

To these add Edmund Kapp, more character-portraitist than caricaturist, the decorative Powys Evans, *Quiz*, and others perhaps too newly arrived to judge of the lasting quality of their talents. And last (but not, I hope, least) the writer, Low, of whom it is advisable only to say with hypocritical modesty that he does his best.

'TRY ZIDEWAYS'

CARRIER : " *Try zideways, Mrs. Jones, try zideways !* "
MRS. JONES : " *Lar, bless 'ee, John, I ain't got no zideways !* "

Drawing by L. Raven Hill

IN HONOUR OF THE BRITISH NAVY
To commemorate the surrender of the German Fleet
Cartoon by Sir Bernard Partridge, 1918

YESTERDAY AND TO-DAY

MANY changes have taken place since Mistress Humphrey hung Gillray's etchings in the window of her shop for sale to passers-by. To-day cartoons find their place chiefly in the daily newspapers. Of weeklies printing cartoons, *Punch* alone survives, the vehicle still for the Tenniel Tradition now become a national institution, carried on with undiminished honour by Bernard Partridge. If, indeed, after the latter's record of achievement over forty years it may not be said now to be the Partridge Tradition.

For some time before Tenniel's retirement in 1900, Partridge had been drawing joke illustrations and theatrical portraits, sober but exhibiting sense of character and humour. When Sambourne succeeded Tenniel, Partridge became "junior" cartoonist, and the work of these two artists contrasted piquantly week by week. In pen technique they were opposites. Sambourne used bold firm lines, but Partridge drew with the finest pens, elaborately shading his careful compositions. Both were essentially honest draughtsmen "of the studio" with no tricks, but while Sambourne often merely suggested, Partridge drew minutest details.

Partridge as cartoonist owes little to his predecessors save the approach and the inherited symbolism, which he soon made his own. The stately but stiff goddesses of Tenniel (which in Sambourne's version had grown womanly but lost no weight) when depicted by Partridge became slim and graceful. The national animals and birds—British Lion, Russian Bear, German Eagle, etc.—became more like the animals one sees at the Zoo.

Partridge's cartooning covers the period which may be called the prelude to the present. A time of rich material. At first overshadowed by Sambourne, who got the cream of the international subject matter, his métier was perhaps too heroic to show to advantage in the knock-about of domestic politics, despite his ability in portraiture. Graceful allegory, like *Homing*, in which pigeons representing the Overseas Dominions are seen returning to *Britannia* ; or classical drama, are more in his line. His most memorable cartoons appeared during the first world war, when he rose to the occasion in his own particular field. *The World's Enemy* shows Kaiser Wilhelm on a battle-torn landscape challenging the Spirit of Carnage with " Who goes there ? " " A friend—your only one," replies the wild figure. Another cartoon pictures the Kaiser confronting King Albert of the Belgians : " You have lost everything," says the Kaiser. "Not my soul," says the King. These impressive cartoons are remembered after twenty-five years, when, wearing a different moustache, history is repeating itself.

Contemporary with Partridge as cartoonist for many years was L. Raven Hill. Those who remember gratefully his joke illustrations of the '90's and onwards will debate whether he was seen at his best in the more specialised field of cartooning ; for Raven Hill was a comic artist as essentially as was Keene, and his talents were not pre-eminently those of a cartoonist.

The comparison with Keene arises naturally since in Raven Hill's earlier work the carefully studied backgrounds, the unity of composition, rich effects of light and shade—to say nothing of the peculiar chuckling humour and the instinctive choice of certain types of jokes—show that the master had a pupil capable of digesting and absorbing his lessons. Had bicycles and motor-cars been invented in Keene's day he would have done just what Raven Hill did with them. If, then, an artist is entitled to be estimated on his best work, undoubtedly Raven Hill must be represented by his famous picture, "*Try zideways, Mrs. Jones, try zideways!*." Or by one of his many sidelights on soldiering and camp-life—say, that of the newly-enlisted yeoman who couldn't get his horse to eat its oats and complains, " Please, sergeant, my 'orse won't

By courtesy of the Artist

'THE MAN WHO LIT HIS CIGAR BEFORE THE ROYAL TOAST'
Drawing by H. M. Bateman

By courtesy of the Artist

'THE PAST MEETS THE PRESENT': JUBILEE DAY ON OLYMPUS'
Cartoon by David Low

The gathering includes such well-known gods as Ramsay MacDonald, Bernard Shaw, Wells,
Maxton, Reith, Beaverbrook, Lloyd George, Barrie, Churchill and C. B. Cochran: also, some
theatre, and lost in the long line, himself

pick up 'is seed." Or by the drunk just passed by a clattering fire-engine who snuffles bitterly after it : " Orright, keep yer 'ot potatoes ! " These are good comic art. There is unforced fun in the drawing.

Naturally, therefore, as a cartoonist he was most at home in the vein of humour, dealing with byplay of home affairs rather than with the drama of nations. The infinitely varied Lloyd George became to him almost what Chamberlain was to F.C.G., and his best cartoons were among those which dealt humorously with the Welsh Wizard. By the cussedness of fate, however, his best remembered cartoon is one of the " serious " kind, published when Lloyd George undertook to solve the shell-shortage problem during the first world war. It represents Ll.G. post-riding the two horses Capital, and Labour drawing the cartload of munitions, and is entitled, *Delivering the Goods*.

The example of *Punch* had inspired emulation overseas. India had *Hindu Punch*, printing cartoons suggestive of Tenniel with Eastern flavouring ; Canada had its *Grip* with drawings by Bengough ; Sydney *Punch* burst forth in Australia, followed, as a reaction, by the *Bulletin*, an illustrated weekly specialising in topical cartoons, political and otherwise. The *Bulletin* had no use for imported traditions, but was a wholly indigenous article reflecting the native freshness of a new land, and its pungent and witty manner of dealing with public affairs was all its own. Here was an ideal nursery for satire and a school of cartoonists and caricaturists grew up around it, just as in France, a generation before, Philipon's " phalanx " —including the great Daumier— had grown up around *Charivari* and *La Caricature*. Two of the most famous *Bulletin* artists, though, were not Australian at all. Phil May (whose work is noted in earlier pages) was English, but he first made his mark in Australia. Livingstone Hopkins, *Hop*, was an American who found that the climates of both Australia and the *Bulletin* suited him. He was a humorist of the Artemus Ward vintage with a quaint drollery in both the invention and the execution of his cartoons.

If the *Bulletin's* cartoonists had influence on the political and social development of Australia, it was *Hop's* pungent fun that had most to do with moulding its sense of humour. As might be expected, in days when Britain used the " colonies " as a kind of ash-can for its ne'er-do-wells, the *Bulletin* was not always pro-English, and *Hop's* cartoons were sometimes scandalously irreverent. What orthodox English spine would not creep at, say, *Hop's* prickling piece of debunking, published on the occasion of the demise of the reigning sovereign, when the pubs of Sydney were shut for two days as a mark of respect : *The Nation Mourns*, showing a thirsty customer with his tongue hanging out waiting on a pub doorstep ? Another *Bulletin* man, Norman Lindsay, Australian-born, is justly more famous beyond Australia as an illustrator than as a cartoonist ; but his work over thirty years on the *Bulletin* is an historical record salted with many excellent cartoons. *The War God Strikes his Gong*, printed at the opening of the first great war, is perhaps his high-water-mark.

ONE MAN IN HIS TIME PLAYS MANY PARTS'
Caricatures of Joseph Chamberlain by F. C. Gould

The cartoonist for the modern newspaper works under very different conditions to those of Gillray's time. The one cartoon a week has become one cartoon a day. The methods of preparing his work are more simple ; but the very efficiency of the machine of which he is a part circumscribes him within the limits of a rigid time-table, and forces him to an endless pursuit of ever-changing headlines.

F. C. Gould, *F.C.G.*, was the first in Britain to contribute a cartoon daily to a newspaper. *F.C.G.'s* talents diverted him from stockbroking to journalism at 36 and he was aided for a great part of his career by sympathetic editorial collaboration. Politically minded and a strong Liberal partisan, his cartoons had a penetrating content that endeared him not only to those who shared his viewpoint but to those who liked a dash of vinegar with their politics. As a draughtsman he began influenced by the Tenniel school, and never quite got rid of a certain wood-block flavour in his penmanship. *F.C.G.* had notable dexterity in original first-hand portraiture, and in many cases his were the originals of what became later the commonly accepted cartoon versions of public men. When lesser men showed with their " brilliant pencils " " the way to draw Chamberlain," for instance, they showed only the way to draw Chamberlain as *F.C.G.* drew him. This unusual ability, together with his clever ideas, his fund of allegory and quickness in finding parallels to current situations in well-known literature, drama and art, well appreciated as they were, rather obscured his talents

42

in drawing. In some quarters, where the relationship between qualities
of line and keys of expression are imperfectly apprehended, *F.C.G.* is remembered, quite unjustly, as a poor draughtsman. The truth is that his drawing
was adequate, fit for its purpose, one with the material. Many of his
cartoons would be not nearly so good were they drawn " better." His most
ambitious work was the *Modern Froissart*, an annual illustrated history
of modern England, in the style of a quaint mediæval chronicle. Foreign
politics he left alone. Joseph Chamberlain and his fiscal policies were *F.C.G.'s*
particular prey. He admitted once that he had drawn Chamberlain in no less
than a hundred guises, ranging over history, mythology and zoology. It was
said that Chamberlain was as proud of his collection of *F.C.G.'s* as of his collection of orchids. *F.C.G.* worked for the *Westminster Gazette*, a newspaper
primarily of opinion. But the expansion of the modern newspaper as a
business enterprise was now under way, with certain consequences to
cartoonists. To accord with the shift towards entertainment, cartoonists
became more numerous and prolific ; but on the other hand the commercial
necessity of not alienating circulation tended to restrict the strong meat
of satire and to encourage facetiousness.

The aggressive Gillray spirit
seemed to have died out of cartooning in Britain when Will Dyson
arrived from Australia to prove that
it had merely been renewing its
youth overseas. Dyson was a
Sydney *Bulletin* portrait caricaturist
who after trying his luck for a year
in London became a cartoonist. In
the weekly *Herald* (now the *Daily
Herald*) he began to offer cartoons
of socialist inspiration, drawn with
an infusion of grotesque macabre
suggesting Continental influences and
containing a sarcastic disrespect for
orthodox standards that was an
emetic for the complaisant. He soon
became the most effective propagan-
dist Labour had—Labour, that is,
not necessarily the Labour Party, for
Dyson was an individualist with
strong ideas and ideals of his own,
who could be caustic about leaders.
On the outbreak of war in 1914 he
rose to great heights. His incisive
cartoons on the efforts of Germany

'GOOD-BYE TO ALL THAT'
Cartoon by Tom Webster

A FANTASY: LABOUR LEADERS AT THEIR DEVOTIONS
Cartoon by Will Dyson

to pervert the gifts of science to destructive purposes (later collected under the title of *Kultur Cartoons*) frequently occupied full-pages in the national daily newspapers. Loaded with meaning and direct appeal, they were powerful in the full sense of the word. To those brought up on the Tenniel tradition, Dyson's strength, under stress, sometimes had a streak of over-caricature. The strong Workingman swelled perhaps too much, his Capitalists were too aggressively fat, and his Devils were too devlish—and too numerous. Devils kept creeping into his cartoons. When in post-war days of " tranquillity " the *Herald* revived to serve a Labour Party now groomed to respectability as His Majesty's Opposition, the editor was moved to shut down on the Devils. Dyson was conjured to play the Party game and flatter the Party leaders, to become tame and " funny." Could the leopard change its spots ? Dyson was a mordant wit, not a " popular " humorist. He retired and it was not until after an interval of some years that he rejoined his old paper once again as cartoonist. But it was a different world with different values and he himself had changed. His heart was no longer in his work, which was insignificant compared with those earlier cartoons which had stamped him as the most distinguished survivor of his day in the earlier tradition of satirical caricature. Contemporary and contrasting with Dyson were W. K. Haselden and *Poy*, pen-name of Percy Fearon, both of whom for many years poured out daily amiable cartoons on social and political affairs respectively. Haselden, working for a newspaper which made a particular appeal to women, was more pre-occupied with the quick expression of his pleasant ideas about manners and modes than with perfection of drawing. *Poy's* most striking characteristic lay hardly in art at all, for he never essayed high flights of draughtsmanship. It was his fertile invention of humorous endearing symbols, mostly in pairs, which gave him pungency in political comment. His *Dux and Drakes, Dilly and Dally, Cuthbert* the Whitehall rabbit, and *Dora* the Defence-of-the-Realm-Act old lady, were in their time national pets. He created *John Citizen*, the representative of the Common Mass, the first variant of the obsolete figure of *John Bull* to win general acceptance. A well-known and characteristic *Poy* cartoon was that which appeared on a particularly disastrous gloomy day during the first great war. It represented *John Citizen* with his mouth spread by a glove-stretcher, entitled, *Smile, Damn You, Smile* !

Although the drawings of Sydney Strube do not in the least resemble those of Cruikshank, the two may be said to be akin in that both have the peculiar flavour of Cockney. Strube is essentially a " popular " humorist, a specialist in extracting a political twist out of current songs and sayings. He is constitutionally too friendly to dip his pen in acid for a cartoon crusade against sin and wickedness. In his cartoons even aggressive dictators are no devilish madmen, but just somewhat mistaken persons. He is completely at one with his multitudinous public, for whose delectation he created the famous *Little Man* to display the good-humoured attitude towards the little troubles of everyday life—especially income tax.

A bird of another roost is Tom Webster, sports cartoonist. The British it is freely admitted, are a nation of sportsmen. That is to say, they have a pronounced capacity for sitting in a grandstand watching someone else play games. Tom Webster, daily reporting the pageant of sport in his lively new manner, filled a long-felt national need and became popular at once. It was

DILLY AND DALLY   JOHN CITIZEN   DUX AND DRAKES
Original drawings by Percy Fearon (*Poy*)

45

AFTER THE RAID
" Is it all right now, Henry? "
" Yes, not even scratched."
Drawing by Sidney Strube, 1941

no longer necessary even to sit in a grandstand, for one could enjoy the sporting life through his eyes over breakfast. Webster's drawing is not drawing in the conventional sense at all, but rather comic pictorial gossip reporting. Ordinarily, more than half of his cartoon is text. He disdains draughtsmanship and banks on undiluted verve and raciness almost entirely. With the aid of freely-sketched caricatures of his butts, not more profound than the circumstances warrant, he carries on sustained personal " gags " which in some cases continue for years and years. His work has extraordinary popularity and he has many imitators— none of whom gets anywhere near him.

To the list might be added the writer, Low, about whose works opinions differ. Since close proximity to the trees proverbially renders the wood invisible, useful comment here must be confined to the remark that at least

46

AND HERE IS SIR ROBERT PIPPIN, TO TELL YOU SOMETHING ABOUT REBUILDING THE
POST-WAR WORLD '
Drawing by Captain Bruce Bairnsfather

the philosophical attitude to, and technical intentions of, his cartoons may be
guessed from the comments expressed in this book.

There are others, new hands discovered by the present war, but these,
too, must await the fullness of time for disentanglement of creative genius from
emulative talent and a proper estimation of their respective contributions to
the fullness of art.

In British Comic Art for a decade after Phil May there were no marked
innovations, most artists being content to follow the footsteps of the big men
of the past with individual variations. Artistic children of Leech, Keene,
du Maurier and May multiplied, preserving traditional forms and styles. If
of these no outstanding personality springs to mind it is because the general
average of proficiency is so much higher. Of many, there is space here to men-

47

tion only George Belcher, influenced by Phil May but the sole survivor to better his master ; Heath Robinson, the mild delineator of the maddest inventions ; and Bruce Bairnsfather, the war comic artist, creator of the immortal *Old Bill*, without whom the first world war certainly never could have been won.

With the grotesque of H. M. Bateman, the British inheritor of Caran D'Ache, master of the " story without words " and of the Embarrassment Situation, came a hint of approaching change. With Kenneth Bird, *Fougasse*, a moderniser of the hieroglyphic method to illustrate the lives and habits of Londoners, came another, even broader. In the recent past has appeared a definite decline in the traditional illustrated-joke form and a return to the pure visual humour of character or situation which needs no words. This is exemplified in the drawings of *Pont* (regrettably dead too soon), a keenly satirical social observer none the worse for his technical naïveté.

Here, arbitrarily, this survey must end, necessarily incomplete. Hogarth's " moral pictures " have become the familiar daily cartoons on public affairs. The crude scrawlings of primitive humorists have become the polished and specialised comic art. In Britain, at least, as befits an aspiring democracy, there is still an appreciation of the need for expression both satirical and urbane, rude and polite. Perhaps the best is still to come.